Where We Live

Homes in the Past

Raintree

Raintree is an imprint of Capstone Global Library Limited, a company incorporated in England and Wales having its registered office at 7 Pilgrim Street, London, EC4V 6LB – Registered company number: 6695582

www.raintreepublishers.co.uk
myorders@raintreepublishers.co.uk

Text © Capstone Global Library Limited 2014
First published in hardback in 2014
Paperback edition first published in 2015
The moral rights of the proprietor have been asserted.

Edited by Daniel Nunn and Abby Colich
Designed by Cynthia Akiyoshi
Picture research by Mica Brancic
Production by Sophia Argyris
Originated by Capstone Global Library
Printed and bound in China at RR Donnelley Asia Printing Solutions

ISBN 978-1-4062-6324-4 (hardback)
17 16 15 14 13
10 9 8 7 6 5 4 3 2 1

ISBN 978-1-4062-6329-9 (paperback)
18 17 16 15 14
10 9 8 7 6 5 4 3 2 1

British Library Cataloguing in Publication Data
Smith, Sian.
   Homes in the past. -- (Where we live)
   1. Dwellings--History--Juvenile literature.
   I. Title II. Series
   643.1'09-dc23

Acknowledgements
We would like to thank the following for permission to reproduce photographs: Alamy pp. 8 (© The National Trust Photolibrary), 20 (© Arny Raedts); Getty Images pp. 7 (Time Life Pictures/Wallace G. Levison), 9 (Comstock Images/Jupiterimages), 10 (George Eastman House/Alfred Holden), 12 (Gamma-Keystone/Keystone-France), 13 (Photographer's Choice/Geri Lavrov), 14 (The Bridgeman Art Library/Wilhelm Kranz), 16 (Archive Photos/Buyenlarge), 17 (The Bridgeman Art Library/John Hauser), 19 (Hulton Archive), 21 (Britain On View/VisitBritain/Rod Edwards), 22 left (Hulton Archive); Shutterstock pp. 11 (© pics721), 18 (© Platslee), 22 right (© Wilm Ihlenfeld); SuperStock pp. 4, 23 bottom (Science and Society), 5, 6 (ClassicStock.com), 15, 23 top (Newberry Library).

Front cover photograph of a medieval castle in Bedzin, Poland, reproduced with permission of Shutterstock (© Pecoid). Back cover photograph of 14th-cebtury Bodiam Castle, East Sussex, reproduced with permission of Shutterstock (© Platslee).

Every effort has been made to contact copyright holders of material reproduced in this book. Any omissions will be rectified in subsequent printings if notice is given to the publisher.

Contents

Homes in the past

People in the past needed homes, just like we do today.

Homes kept people safe from the weather.

Homes gave people a safe place to sleep.

Homes gave people a safe place to cook and eat.

Then and now

pot

Long ago, homes did not have bathrooms. People used pots or toilets outside.

8

Homes today have bathrooms.

Long ago, people used candles for light.

electric light

fridge freezer

Homes today have electric lights and fridge freezers.

Long ago, many homes were small.
Families had to share rooms.

Many homes today are bigger.
Many people have their own rooms.

Types of home in the past

At first, people lived in caves.

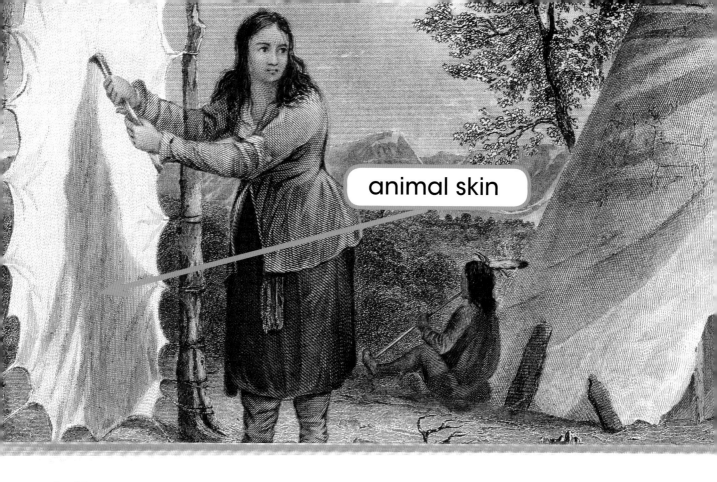

animal skin

After that, people used different materials to make homes.

Some homes were made from mud.

brick

Some homes were made from brick.

Some homes were made from stone.

Some homes were made from wood.

The first homes made from wood
did not have many rooms.

Some homes that were built long ago are still used today.

Same or different?

A home in the past

A home today

How do these two homes look the same? How do these two homes look different?

Picture glossary

material what something is made from. Wood and mud are types of material.

past something that happened before today

Index

Photograph information

Here is some information about the photographs in this book: p. 4 shows a miner and his family, North Wales, 1931; p. 5 was taken in the United States; p. 6 was taken in the 1940s; p. 7 was taken in 1920s; p. 8 shows the Victorian Room in Castle Coole Northern Ireland; p. 10 was taken in 1898; p. 12 shows a family in Ohio, United States in the 1900s; p. 14 shows cavemen during the Ice Age; p. 15 is from the American Aboriginal Portfolio, 1853; p. 16 shows a Navaho hogan, United States, circa 1905; p. 17 shows a Pueblo village in 1900; p. 18 shows the 14th-century Bodiam Castle, East Sussex; p. 19 shows a settler's cabin in Rio de la Mancis, North America, circa 1870; p. 21 was taken in Much Hadham, England; p. 22 (left) was taken in Norris Green, England in 1860.

Notes for parents and teachers

Ask the children what we mean when we talk about the past. What do the children think homes were like a long time ago? List things they think were the same about homes in the past and things they think were different. Read the book together to find out if they were right. Ask the children why they think the picture on page 14 is a drawing and not a photograph, and explain that a really long time ago cameras had not been invented. Tell the children that many of the photographs showing homes in the past were taken about 100 years ago. Look through these together and write a list of questions the children would like answered about what it was like to live in a home 100 years ago. Choose a child or adult who can pretend they are from that time to provide the answers.